Ms T

May God Bless You!

Dakota E. Lee

hesays shesays

Lessons about love and relationships

Dakota E. Lee

THREE:LADIES
PUBLISHING, L.L.C.

DENVER

Copyright © 2003 by Dakota E. Lee

All rights reserved.
No part of this book may be reproduced in any form
or by any means without permission in writing from the author,
except for brief quotations embodied in critical articles and reviews.

For information, contact
Three Ladies Publishing, L.L.C.
9123 E. Mississippi Ave., Suite 13-203
Denver, CO 80231
www.threeladiespublishing.com

He Says She Says: Lessons about love and relationships. -- 1st ed.
LCCN: 2003091705
ISBN: 0-9728559-3-9

Production Management by
Paros Press
1551 Larimer Street, Suite 1301   Denver, CO 80202
303-893-3332   www.parospress.com

BOOK DESIGN BY SCOTT JOHNSON

Printed in the United States of America
1 3 5 7 9 10 8 6 4 2

I was sitting alone in my room

the night after I broke up with one of the most extraordinary women any man could ever hope to meet. Unfortunately, I had been too immature and self-absorbed, and I was unable to communicate my love for her as she had done for me. After much thought, I grabbed a pen and paper and began writing the things I wished she knew; then I wrote the things I thought she wished I knew. The result was more than 30 pages of notes about love, relationships and life that would eventually become this book. I decided to share it with the world in the hope that it might save a relationship, open the lines of communication or create a healthy debate. I would like to thank her for making me aware of my relationship issues – issues that ultimately made me want to be a better man and write this book.

I know there is much that I have missed or was unable to include in this edition. If you have thoughts you would like to see in my next edition, e-mail them to **dakota@threeladiespublishing.com**.

To all of the couples of the world, love with hope and not fear.

Best regards,
Dakota E. Lee

*This book is dedicated
to the Three Ladies who raised me,
loved me unconditionally and supported all my endeavors.
Mattie S. Williams, Frances M. Lee, and Joyce A. Lee.*

*You wonderful ladies have always made the sacrifices
necessary for me to have the best life possible
and for that I thank you.*

*The most important thing all of you taught me
is to put my faith in God, knowing that He
will never forsake me or leave me alone.*

*To my Dad, my brothers and my sister,
continue to have faith in God and His divine will.*

*To Adai, you are truly
one of my greatest blessings.*

*he***says**

Relationship Do's & Don'ts

Do respect her opinions,
even if you don't agree.

Don't be overly concerned
about her romantic past.

Do set financial goals with your mate
and beware of women with
uncontrollable spending habits.

Do focus on what you can control
in your relationship and let go
of the things you can't control.

Don't seek traits from an old lover
in a new lover.

Don't be afraid to admit
that being in love is scary.

Do assess the good and bad
of your relationships, then learn from it.

Don't ever feel pressured
to get married.

Don't judge her too early
because her true character
will emerge over time.

Don't forget to be her friend
and her lover.

Do analyze the habits of couples
with good marriages and relationships.

Don't turn against your mate
when things get painful in the relationship.

*he*says

Don't attract a woman
under false pretenses.

Don't wait too long
to give her the ring.

Do make her number one
on your to do list.

Don't become complacent in your relationship or marriage.

Don't wait for a special day

to show her how special she is.

If you don't like to date

women with children and she has them,

don't make an exception for her

because she's beautiful.

Do support her

as much as she supports you.

Don't expect her to come back

when you're wrong.

Don't assume that

she'll never cheat on you.

Do be prepared to argue

when you feel you're right.

Don't assume that you know
everything about her.

Do be careful when meeting women
if you're drunk or have your beer goggles on.

Don't give a woman
too much too quickly.

Don't be afraid of successful,

famous or wealthy women –

they're frequently the loneliest.

Do be decisive

when making plans with a woman.

Don't ever think

a woman is too good for you.

he says

Do learn to be tolerant

of her nagging habits.

Don't take her love

for granted.

Do be strong

but flexible.

Don't get married

or stay with her

for the wrong reasons.

Don't let one woman

make you hate all women.

Do expect

the best of her.

Do listen to a group of women

when they are talking about men.

Do learn to avoid the mistakes

you've made in the past.

Don't be intimidated

by aggressive and assertive women.

Do put her needs before your own

when you're in love.

hesays

Do date an older woman once –
she'll teach you a lot about women,
life, sex and possibly love.

Don't become involved
with women at work.

Don't always go out
with intentions of meeting a woman.

Don't ignore her plea

to spend more time together.

Honesty is the key

to gaining a woman's respect.

Don't doubt your ability

to make a woman happy.

Don't let too many good women

pass you by.

Don't go through life

without loving.

Don't marry a woman

who hasn't been one of your best friends.

Don't try to

fix everything.

Sometimes, just listen.

Do choose a good woman

over one who's merely beautiful.

Do learn to control

your visual appetite.

Do try to be unselfish

when you're in a relationship.

Do be honest about other women

you may be seeing when you become

involved with someone new.

Do be willing

to listen.

Don't cheat on her

if you love her.

Don't reveal all of your feelings
at the start of a relationship.

Do date women who enrich your life
and who cherish you.

Don't let your individual goals
prevent you from moving forward
in a relationship that's valuable to you.

Don't be afraid to settle down

with just one woman.

Don't become seriously involved

with a woman who left another man

to be with you.

Do try to maintain

a good credit rating.

Don't feel pressured to buy her

a huge ring when the time comes.

Don't be afraid to love

and be loved.

Don't try to make up for past injustices

with your current relationship.

Don't make decisions based solely on her happiness.

Don't become seriously involved
when you're on the rebound
from someone you truly loved.

Don't be afraid
of rejection.

Don't underestimate the value
of pillow talk.

*he***says**

Matters of the Heart

Women believe that most men

lie and cheat.

Each broken relationship leaves her

with more emotional baggage.

Women are often puzzled

by men's sexual attitudes and behaviors.

Women are often afraid to say "no" to sex for fear that a man will lose interest.

Independent and self-assured women won't stand for being mistreated.

All women are attracted to bad boys but smart women marry good boys.

Don't put anything past a woman

when it comes to matters of the heart.

Having good conversations with a woman

is the way to her heart.

Women need to be loved and desired

for more than just their sex appeal.

A woman will give you time

to make a relationship work.

A woman's body is

her most prized possession.

When a woman has had enough,

there's nothing you can say or do

to change her mind.

he says

Women want a man
who is financially secure.

Women value quality time with their partners
more than money and things.

Women are attracted to men who have goals,
dreams and aspirations.

Women

remember

everything.

*he***says**

Women like men who

make them smile, feel good,

and who are willing to try new things.

Be attentive when she's trying

to have a discussion with you.

Women have a difficult time

distinguishing the difference between

love and lust.

Women always know

when you're lying.

Women love to talk about their lives

– be prepared to listen.

Women are very strong, tenacious and

unforgiving when they choose to be.

hesays

Women believe men

don't know how to commit.

Women love men who have

the mental strength and courage to admit

when they are wrong and apologize.

It's the little things

that are big with women.

Never underestimate
women. They are just as capable
of dishonesty and deceit as men.

When women don't have all the answers,

they ask questions.

Women love more

than they lust.

he says

Women often equate

sex with love.

Women talk about men

as much as men talk about women.

When a woman totally dumbfounds you,

talk to your mother about it.

Plan your life with her as much as you plan your bachelor party.

he says

Women forgive

but they don't forget.

There's no good reason

for cheating on a woman.

Relationships need

a spiritual foundation.

Your partner should inspire,

not impair you.

All love and relationships

will experience crisis.

You can't make her happy

if you're not happy with yourself.

*he*says

When you find the woman

you want to spend the rest of your life with,

your work really begins.

Unresolved personal baggage

destroys relationships.

Sometimes there's just too much history

for a relationship to succeed.

You have no control

over love.

You must let go of past relationships

to be open to new ones.

If you are looking for love and cannot find it,

review the places you have been looking.

he says

Financial issues
can ruin a relationship.

Money can never replace
the quality time you spend with her.

A woman scorned
will make your life a living hell.

Women tend to think

with their hearts

and not their heads.

hesays

You'll rarely win arguments

with women.

It's not all about you

when it comes to your relationship.

Life isn't fair

and neither is love.

You'll never

understand women.

One lie

leads to more lies.

Love requires

patience.

he says

If you can't trust her
you don't need her.

Good love often comes
after bad love.

Relationships require
a leap of faith.

Relationships don't have to be

a hindrance to personal goals.

You can't chase skirts

all of your life.

Love isn't always

convenient.

he says

No woman is perfect,

no love is perfect and

no relationship is perfect.

In love and relationships,

things won't always go your way.

Bad love and relationships

happen to good people.

Women want

emotional intimacy

to precede sexual intimacy.

hesays

Love will make you feel like

you're losing your mind.

Pick

your battles.

All cheaters

eventually get caught.

There is more to a good relationship

than just good sex.

Work harder on your inner self

than on your outer self.

If you leave her alone at your house

she's going to snoop.

hesays

Money without someone special

to share it with isn't worth having.

Cheating and lying will destroy

even the strongest love.

You'll never stop finding

other women attractive.

Being handsome may get you in the door,

but intelligence will keep you there.

Drinking makes men

truthful, talkative and horny.

Spending time with her

shouldn't be a chore.

hesays

The right woman will make you want to be a better man.

There will be good and bad times in any relationship.

"Booty calls" may mean more to her than just sex.

Women cheat when their emotional needs aren't being met.

hesays

There's no way to be in a relationship

and single at the same time.

Just because your friends cheat

doesn't mean you have to as well

– do what you know is right.

Avoid telling her you've never been faithful

in any of your past relationships.

Don't be too much of a man

to tell her you love her.

Learn to compromise with your woman.

If all you want is a

physical relationship, tell her.

Let her know how much – or how little

– she means to you.

he says

During arguments, focus on what is right
instead of who is right.

Never ask a woman
how many sexual partners she's had.

There's never a good time
to give a woman bad news.

A woman wants all of you.

Discuss finances before you get married.

Never say anything bad about her family.

Identify what you want in a woman.

he says

Do return home if you leave
during an argument.

Stop complaining and start addressing
the things that you're complaining about
in your relationship.

Don't be afraid to talk about
your relationship baggage with your mate.

*he***says**

Between the Sheets

*he*says

Make love
after a fight or argument.

Never sleep with a woman
you wouldn't want to be
the mother of your child.

Set the mood with candles,
incense and soft music when making love.

If she asks you for something

specific sexually, give it to her.

Concentrate on being the best

you've ever been instead of

worrying about being her best ever.

Always have access

to a condom.

hesays

Things will change

after you sleep with her.

Be particular about the women

with whom you have sex.

Ask her

if she is satisfied sexually.

Share your sexual fantasies

with her.

Try to stay awake

for at least 20 minutes after sex.

Alcohol doesn't improve

your sexual performance.

hesays

Love-making is about more

than just the physical.

Learn how to be

a good lover.

Introduce her immediately when

you run into another woman you know.

Women believe that
men do everything
to get them and
very little to keep them.

he says

Keep all promises
you make to her.

Encourage her to have hobbies
that don't always include you.

When you care about a woman
be sincere about getting to know her,
her goals and her interests.

Don't always ask women

for their phone numbers –

give them your card and ask them to call you.

When out in public with your woman,

especially at a club, bar, or social event,

make it a point to notice only her.

Send cards, flowers

and most importantly hand written notes.

hesays

Be willing to give
as good as you get.

When she says "we need to talk,"
it usually means you're not meeting her needs,
you're taking her for granted
or that she's leaving you.

Your love for an ex
won't go away overnight.

Do buy her sexy lingerie,

prepare her a bath, and give her

a massage at least once a month.

Don't mistake good sex

for a good woman.

When mingling with a group of women,

be patient. If one of them likes you,

she'll let you know or

one of her girlfriends will tell you.

he says

Once a month,

do something with her

that she likes to do even if you don't.

Things are not always

what they seem with women.

If love always leaves your life,

you may be the cause.

Women may use sex

to control you.

When she wants you close to her,

it doesn't necessarily mean

that she wants to have sex.

When she truly loves you,

she'll do anything for you.

hesays

Don't expect to find

Superwoman

– you're not Superman.

shesays

Don't expect

to find Superman —

you're not Superwoman.

Men are

extremely visually stimulated.

Be suspicious of any man

who doesn't make eye contact when

you ask tough or serious questions.

If he loves you

he'll ask for sexual exclusivity.

shesays

If he doesn't rush to sleep with you,
don't panic. It usually means
that he likes and respects you.

If he cares about you he won't share details
about your sex life with his friends.

Don't deny the signs a man gives you
when he's cheating.

Men are impatient
when it comes to sex.

Take note of his behavior in a room full
of beautiful women. If he only notices you,
then you've got a keeper.

It's difficult for men to go without sex
for long periods of time.

she*says*

Be careful what you tell your friends about your sex life.

Never ask him how many women he has slept with. The number is probably higher than you'd like.

When he stops wanting to have sex with you, there's someone else.

Leave any man
who hits you.

You'll know in your heart
if he doesn't love you anymore –
your heart doesn't lie.

If he tells you he's not good at relationships,
or that you deserve someone better,
he wants to break up with you.

she**says**

There are men who believe they can be
in love with you, be married to you,
and still sleep with other women.

If he really cares for you
he will put you first, be faithful to you and
do whatever it takes to keep you happy.

If he has children but doesn't take care of them,
don't get involved with him.

Men sometimes sleep with women

they don't find attractive.

Don't be afraid to ask him

if he's been tested for AIDS

before you have sex with him.

A man will tell you he loves you

in order to have sex.

shesays

Don't be afraid to approach a man you find
attractive – men enjoy this tremendously.

Do engage him in
pillow talk after sex.

Let him know
when he's not pleasing you sexually.

Flirt with him even after he's yours.

You may have to

teach him

the value of foreplay.

she**says**

Be careful not to confuse
love with lust.

Men can and will have sex
without emotional attachment.

Men thrive on the thrill of the chase,
overcoming a woman's objections
and winning her heart.

The majority of men you sleep with
will disappoint you.

Good sex is a vital part
of a relationship.

Expect him to change
once you have sex with him.

shesays

Don't feel compelled

to sleep with every man you date.

No matter how good the sex,

leave him if he doesn't treat you right.

Don't expect the first time to be very good.

He'll probably be too excited and nervous

to last very long.

Always carry a condom in your purse;
don't depend on him to have one.

Some men use sex
as a sleeping pill.

Never sleep with a man you wouldn't
want to be the father of your child.

shesays

Having sex can be
a great way to make up.

Always have pretty lingerie and wear it often.

His needs in the bedroom will change
constantly; sometimes he'll want you
to be dominant, and sometimes he'll want you
to be submissive. The best way to find out
what he wants is to ask.

she says

Between the Sheets

shesays

Remember

to argue fairly.

Never tell him you love him

if you don't.

Never argue with him in public

or in the presence of family and friends.

If he lies in the beginning,
he'll always lie.

If he doesn't take you out in public,
he's hiding something.

His attention won't last
if he doesn't have feelings for you.

she says

Always speak your mind

but do so carefully, honestly and tactfully.

Don't be afraid to discuss

your emotional baggage with your man.

Try, wear or use whatever he buys you

as soon as possible.

Always ask him
if he has a girlfriend or wife.

Never ask him to buy you something
you can't afford to buy yourself.

Talk with him about the issues you share
before you talk with anyone else.

shesays

A man's true character
will emerge over time.

Avoid telling him everything about you
or your past relationships.

Two-way communication is essential
to any good relationship.

During arguments

try to focus on

what is right rather than

who is right.

shesays

Any man can give you a baby.

Only a real man can be a father.

No relationship

can be built on lies.

True love

is reciprocal.

You can't hurry love, even when
your biological clock is ticking.
Building a strong relationship takes time.

The more people you have in your relationship
the more difficult it is.

Relationships require more time,
energy and effort than any job.

she*says*

Relationships need
a spiritual foundation.

If you decide to give him a second chance,
be careful. Your reunion won't necessarily lead
to marriage or a lasting relationship.

Your girlfriends aren't always right about men,
especially the ones who are single.

Just because you got hurt last time
doesn't mean you'll get hurt the next time.

Your parents will remember
everything negative you say about him.

Once the trust is gone,
the relationship is over.

she**says**

It's not a good idea

to go through his personal belongings.

If he isn't who you want him to be

when you meet, he won't become

who you want him to be over time.

A good male friend can give you insight

into what men really think and

why they act the way they do.

The older you get,
the less time you have
for meaningless
relationships.

shesays

A good man will stand by you
through good and bad times.

Once you say "I do," the real work begins;
the road to forever is paved
with good times and bad.

A broken heart will mend,
but a broken spirit won't.

There will be one man in your life
who will destroy your faith in men;
there will be another
who will restore your faith in men.

Love has
many moods.

Pick your battles.

she*says*

There is a difference

between what he wants

and what he needs.

Focus on what you can control

about your relationship and let go

of what you can't control.

Relationships

have lulls and ruts.

You can only learn
so much about yourself
by yourself.

Anger can destroy
a relationship.

Money issues
can ruin a marriage or a relationship;
set financial goals with your mate.

shesays

Real love is nothing

like a romance novel.

Define and set

clear relationship boundaries.

Develop a realistic picture

of what Mr. Right looks like.

A sure way

to turn him off

is to complain all the time.

shesays

Men use alcohol to build up courage

to do and say things

they wouldn't normally do.

Men tend to handle infidelity

harder than women.

A man can lie so often

it becomes easy.

If he loves you

he'll put your needs before his own.

Men believe the quickest solution

is the best solution.

Men talk in riddles

about their true feelings and intentions.

shesays

Men marry women they believe

will be good mothers.

Some men

will always cheat.

Instead of just listening,

men try to fix things when there's a problem.

A man can think something for a long time
before he communicates it to you.

Men want second and third chances
but don't like to give them.

Men are attracted to women
who don't need them.

shesays

Men believe women
don't often cheat.

A man never wants to be
the first to say it's over.

Men are good at responding
to expressed expectations.

When he says,

"Nothing's wrong,"

Something's wrong.

she*says*

Men rarely go through a woman's belongings,

because they have no desire to find

something that may hurt them.

Know that men lust more

than they love.

Men don't

forgive easily.

Men are easily confused
and quick to run from confusion.

Men need help remembering
important dates, events and anniversaries.

Men are rarely truly single –
they generally have someone,
even if it's just a sex partner.

shesays

Men are terrible at long distance relationships

because of the temptation to be

with other women.

Men will agree with you or lie to you

to avoid an argument.

If he's not ready to settle down,

he'll leave you even though he loves you.

A large percentage
of men cheat.

Listen to what your father and brothers
tell you about men.

Men believe their hearts are fragile
so they protect them at all costs.

shesays

Most men don't realize a good woman
until she is gone.

If he thinks he can't make you happy
he'll slowly distance himself from you.

Men expect women to be
strong but emotional,
aggressive but tender, in charge but flexible.

Men are the first to get bored in a relationship and the last to address it.

she*says*

Men shy away from high-maintenance women.
They may play for a while, but they won't stay
if they think it will cost too much.

When men fall in love,
they fall hard.

If you keep treating him badly
he'll find another woman.

Most men choose brains over looks
in the long run, but along the way they'll
enjoy women with looks absent of brains.

It takes men longer
to learn about love.

Too much free time isn't good for men –
this is generally when they get into trouble.

shesays

If he really cares for you,

he shouldn't be afraid to meet your parents.

Don't let a man you're dating

see you drunk.

Men prefer quick break ups

with very few tears.

Most men don't know

that communication, caring and honesty

result in true intimacy.

Men aspire to have

uncomplicated lives.

Even good men

lie sometimes.

shesays

Men are often self-centered,

even when in a relationship.

Men are not

good listeners.

Men believe that women love hard

and love blindly.

Do praise your man
for his everyday
contributions and
achievements.

shesays

Men hate to

argue.

A sure way to impress him

is to speak knowledgeably about sports.

If he wants to spend time with you

he will.

When he does or says something
that hurts your feelings,
he probably won't realize it.

The company he keeps
says a lot about him.

Men want and need
positive reinforcement from women.

shesays

Men tend not to admit

their relationship fears.

Men try to hide

their relationship baggage.

Men believe

what women don't know

won't hurt them.

His jealousy
is about control.

Men will try to get away
with everything they can.

Men view love
as a burden.

shesays

Men will consistently

do and say dumb things.

Most men are not forthright

about their intentions.

Men believe women have been conditioned

to make relationships work.

she says

Matters of the Heart

shesays

Don't try to be perfect

to attract the man you want.

Do take time to listen

to a group of men discussing women.

Don't try to salvage a relationship

by getting pregnant.

Do believe

in a man's actions

and not his words.

shesays

Do make sure he knows the difference

between courting and dating.

Don't expect one man

to make up for other men's injustices.

Don't base your decisions

solely on his happiness.

Do love him, but don't lose yourself
nor let a man's love define who you are.

Don't try to control him.
You'll only push him away.

Don't always go out
with the intention of meeting a man.

Do make all first dates lunch.

she*says*

Don't love him so much
that his lies become the truth.

Don't overlook the man who listens to you
and is always there when you need him —
sometimes love is closer than you think.

Do try to be an optimist
about love and relationships.

Do plan the rest

of your life with him

as much as you plan

your wedding to him.

shesays

Do seek advice on love and relationships

from the right people.

Do forgive him

before you end the relationship.

Do allow yourself to be sad and angry

after a bad relationship.

When the bad consistently outweighs the good,

it is time to let go.

Do give him space,

let him be a couch potato once in a while.

Don't point out your perceived flaws

or shortcomings to a man.

Do learn to cook.

shesays

Don't let him blame his foul behavior
on his friends.

Don't let old baggage destroy
a chance at new love but do be able
to identify your relationship baggage.

Don't dwell on the past.
Always know how to move forward.

Don't be
"the other woman."

Do give men with children
or blue collar jobs a chance.

Don't take his money or heart
if you don't like him.

she*says*

Don't expect more from him
than you expect from yourself.

Don't let your miserable single friends
taint your happiness – misery loves company.

Don't waste time and energy feeling guilty –
pinpoint problems in your relationship
and work to solve them.

Don't let your judgment

be eclipsed by

your desire to be loved.

she**says**

Don't marry him if he's not
one of your best friends.

Do keep men around who are positive,
nurturing and complimentary. You may not
believe what they say but it's nice to hear.

Don't spend a lot of time alone
when suffering from a broken heart.

Do be able to identify
what you want in a man.

Don't judge all men by one man's actions
but judge each man on his own merits.

Do know when to stand firm
and when to compromise.

shesays

Don't compromise your
feelings, morals and goals
to hold a relationship together.

Don't allow the man to set
all of the relationship rules.

Don't wait on any man
for too long.

Do always work at

constructive conflict resolution.

Don't let outside issues

– or people –

affect your relationship.

Don't make excuses for him

treating you badly.

shesays

Don't be blinded by lust

when what you need is love.

Don't seek an old lover's traits

in a new lover.

Don't shift blame

during an argument.

*she***says**

Relationship Do's & Don'ts